DATE DUE

A ROOKIE BIOGRAPHY

FRANZ JOSEPH HAYDN

Great Man of Music

By Carol Greene

 CHILDRENS PRESS®
CHICAGO

This book is for Ann Marie Ruhlin,
who makes many people happy with music.

Franz Joseph Haydn (1732-1809)

Library of Congress Cataloging-in-Publication Data

Greene, Carol.
  Franz Joseph Haydn : great man of music / by Carol Greene.
    p.   cm. — (A Rookie biography)
  Includes index.
  ISBN 0-516-04260-2
  1. Haydn, Joseph, 1732-1809—Juvenile literature. 2. Composers—
Austria—Biography—Juvenile literature. [1. Haydn, Joseph, 1732-1809.
2. Composers.] I. Title. II. Series: Greene, Carol. Rookie biography.
ML3930.H3G7   1994
780′.92—dc20
  [B]   93-37522
                                                           CIP
                                                         AC MN

Franz Joseph Haydn
was a real person.
He was born in 1732.
He died in 1809.
Haydn wrote many pieces
of beautiful music,
including 104 symphonies.
This is his story.

TABLE OF CONTENTS

Franz Joseph Haydn was born in this house in Rohrau, Austria.

Chapter 1

A Little Musician

The moon and stars shone down
on tiny Rohrau, Austria.
The day's work was done.
In their home, the Haydn family
sat around the fireplace.

Papa Mathias played
folk songs on his harp.
Mama Maria and
sister Franziska sang.

Young Joseph used sticks to make a pretend violin.

Little Joseph sang too.
He sang very well.
But he wanted to do more.
So he rubbed a stick
across a piece of wood.
That was his violin, he said.

One day, Cousin Franck
visited the Haydns.
He heard Joseph sing
and saw him play
his pretend violin.

"Let Joseph come to Hainburg,"
said Cousin Franck.
"He can live with my family,
go to school,
learn more about music,
and sing in the church choir."

Mama did not want him to go.
Joseph was not yet six.
But she knew it would
be best for him.

So Joseph went to Hainburg.
The Franck family was poor.
He didn't get enough to eat.
Cousin Franck beat him.
But Joseph learned music
and that made him happy.

He learned to play
a real violin
and the clavier.
(A clavier is like a piano.)
He even played the kettledrum.
And, of course, he sang.

Reutter offers to take Joseph to Vienna to study.

Time went by.
One day an important man
from the city of Vienna
heard Joseph sing in church.
The man's name was Reutter.
He led the choir at
St. Stephen's Cathedral.

"You shall come with me!"
he told Joseph.

St. Stephen's Cathedral, Vienna, Austria

A street in old Vienna in 1786, and Vienna (top right) as it looks today, with the spires of St. Stephen's in the distance

So when Joseph was eight,
he went to Vienna.
He lived in a house
next to the cathedral,
with Reutter, some other men,
and five other choirboys.

11

Young Joseph learned much about music from Reutter

Once again, Joseph
didn't get enough to eat.
But he studied music
and made music every day.

The choir sang in church.
They sang for plays.
They sang for city holidays
and for important parties.

The boys liked the parties.
They got free food.

Joseph sang with the choir
for nine years.
But he was growing up.
His voice was changing.

One day in church,
Joseph looked at the pigtail
on the wig of the boy
in front of him.

Joseph had new scissors.
He knew he shouldn't—
but he cut off that pigtail.

Reutter was furious.
He beat Joseph
in front of everyone.
Then he threw Joseph
out of the choir.

Chapter 2

Hard Years

Joseph was 17 years old.
He carried three old shirts
and one old coat.
He had no money
and nowhere to go.

So he spent a long cold night
on a bench outdoors.

But in the morning,
Joseph heard a friendly hello.
It was Spangler,
a man from another choir.

Spangler lived with his wife
and baby son in a little attic.
He said Joseph could stay
in a corner of his attic.
Joseph moved in.

Joseph sang and played the violin in
the streets to make money for food.

The next years were hard.

Joseph gave music lessons.

He played music in the streets.

At last he got his own room.

But he was often cold and hungry.

Joseph's parents wanted him
to come home and become
a Roman Catholic priest.

Joseph felt close to God.
But he didn't want
to be a priest.
He wanted to be a musician.

So he taught himself
to write music.
Other musicians helped him.
Then Count von Morzin gave him a job.
Joseph would write music
and lead the count's orchestra.

An oil painting of Franz Joseph Haydn

By that time, Joseph was 27.
He wanted to get married.
He loved a girl named Therese,
but she became a nun.
So Joseph married
her sister, Maria, instead.

That was a mistake.
Joseph and Maria
didn't love each other.
They were never happy together.

Then Joseph got a new job
with the Esterházy family.
That changed his life.

Haydn meeting Prince Esterházy

Chapter 3

Life in the Country

The Esterházy family
had a castle in
the town of Eisenstadt.
They also built
a palace called Esterház
out in the country.

The Esterházy
castle in
Eisenstadt,
where
Joseph Haydn
wrote many
of his works

Haydn and other musicians practicing his music

Many musicians worked
for the family.
Franz Joseph Haydn was
in charge of them all.
He also played instruments
and wrote music.

It was a huge job,
but just right for Haydn.
He wrote music for singers
and music for instruments,
big pieces, little pieces,
all kinds of music.

Portrait of
Joseph Haydn
in 1792

Haydn was good with people too.
He took care of his musicians
and they called him "Papa."
Haydn liked that.
He and Maria had
no children of their own.

When he wasn't working,
Haydn played with
the children around Esterház.
He had a puppet theater
and liked to fish.

Haydn (seated at left) gathered with other famous composers in Vienna.

As the years went by,
the Esterházys spent more
and more time at their country palace.
Sometimes that bothered Haydn.
He wanted to be with
musicians in Vienna too.

Empress Maria Theresa of Austria

But many important people
visited Esterház,
even Empress Maria Theresa.
She liked Haydn's music.

Sheet music for a composition by Joseph Haydn

People began to take
Haydn's music back to Vienna
and to other cities in Europe.
Haydn was becoming famous.
But he didn't know it—yet.

Mozart (right) and Haydn were lifelong friends.

Chapter 4

The Great Man

At last Haydn began
to learn how famous he was.
People from other countries
paid him to write music.
Young musicians asked
to study with him.

One young musician
was very special to Haydn.
His name was Mozart.
Haydn called him
"the greatest composer I know."

Then one morning,
while Haydn was in Vienna,
a stranger came to see him.

"I am Salomon
from London," he said.
"I have come for you."

Salomon had great plans
for Haydn in London.
But Haydn's friends thought
he was too old for the trip.

Portrait of
Joseph Haydn
in 1785

London, England

Haydn didn't agree.

He was 58 and he felt fine.

So off to London he went

and had a wonderful time.

31

The German composer George Frideric Handel (1685-1759) lived in London from 1712 until his death.

He played in and led orchestras.
He wrote beautiful music.
He heard other people's music.
When he heard Handel's
"Hallelujah" chorus, he cried.

"He is the master
of us all," said Haydn.

Haydn stayed in London
for a year and a half.
Sometimes he felt tired.
But he felt happy too.

Then he went back
to Vienna for a while.
He taught a young man
called Beethoven.

Ludwig van
Beethoven (1770-1827)
was a great
German composer.

But soon Haydn took
his godson, Elssler,
and hurried back to London.

Haydn wrote and played
and listened to music there
for another year and a half.
When he left at last,
he had a talking parrot
and a head full of ideas
for more music.

Chapter 5

Papa Haydn

In London, Haydn heard
some of Handel's big pieces
for singers and orchestra.
Now he wanted to write
music like that too.

Singers perform *The Improvised Meeting*, an opera written by Haydn.

A performance of Haydn's *The Creation* at Old University, Vienna

So he settled down
in Vienna and began to
work on *The Creation*.
It was one of the
best pieces he ever wrote.
People loved it.

Portrait of Joseph Haydn

They loved Haydn too.
He led many concerts.
He even wrote a new
national anthem for Austria.

And he went on teaching.
Haydn was always kind
to young musicians.
They still called him "Papa."

When Haydn was 68,
his wife died.
Soon he began to slow down.
He had ideas for new music.
But he wasn't strong enough
to work on them.

Haydn lived in a house
in a suburb of Vienna.
He liked to work in his garden
and play with neighborhood children.
Many people came to see him.

Soldiers of France and Austria fighting a battle

But Austria and France
were at war.
That made Haydn sad.

One day, a French soldier
came to visit Haydn.
The soldier sang
a part of *The Creation*.

Then both men cried
and hugged each other.
They knew that music
is more important than war.

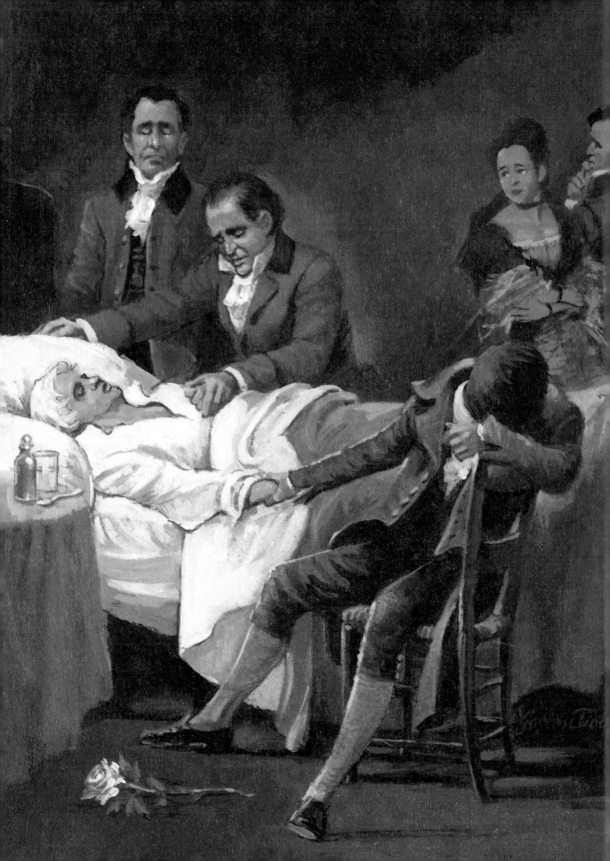

As time went by,
Haydn grew weaker and weaker.
His godson, Elssler,
and servants took care of him.

"Cheer up, children!"
he kept telling them.
"I'm all right."

But on May 31, 1809,
Franz Joseph Haydn
died quietly in his bed.
He was 77.

Haydn died in this room (above). He is buried
in the town of Eisenstadt (below).

Haydn believed that
he wrote his music for God.
But, he said, he saw
so many sad people.
He hoped his music would make
some of them feel happy.

It did.
It still does.

Important Dates

1732   March 31—Born in Rohrau, Austria, to Maria and Mathias Haydn

1738   Went to Hainburg, Austria

1740   Went to St. Stephen's Cathedral, Vienna

1749   Left St. Stephen's

1760   Married Maria Keller

1761   Began working for Esterházy family

1790   Left for first London visit

1794   Left for second London visit

1809   May 31—Died in Gumpendorf, Austria

INDEX

Page numbers in boldface type indicate illustrations.

PHOTO CREDITS

ABOUT THE AUTHOR

Carol Greene has degrees in English literature and musicology. She has worked in international exchange programs, as an editor, and as a teacher of writing. She now lives in Webster Groves, Missouri, and writes full-time. She has published more than 100 books, including those in the Rookie Biographies series.

ABOUT THE ILLUSTRATOR

Of Cajun origins, Steven Gaston Dobson was born and raised in New Orleans, Louisiana. He attended art school in the city and worked as a newspaper artist on the *New Orleans Item*. After serving in the Air Force during World War II, he attended the Chicago Academy of Fine Arts in Chicago, Illinois. Before switching to commercial illustration, Mr. Dobson won the Grand Prix in portrait painting from the Palette and Chisel Club. In addition to his commercial work, Steven taught illustration at the Chicago Academy of Fine Arts and night school classes at LaGrange High School. In 1987, he moved to Englewood, Florida where he says "I am doing something that I have wanted to do all of my 'art life,' painting interesting and historic people."